For my mum, Lynn, and my sist‹

We three Peas x

THE EMMA PRESS

First published in the UK in 2020 by the Emma Press Ltd

ISBN 978-1-912915-38-5

A CIP catalogue record of this book is available from the British Library.

Printed and bound in the UK by The Holodeck, Birmingham.

The Emma Press is an independent publisher dedicated to producing beautiful, thought-provoking books. It was founded in Winnersh in 2012 by Emma Dai'an Wright, and is now based in Birmingham. The Emma Press publishes themed poetry anthologies, single-author poetry and fiction chapbooks and books for children, with a growing list of translations. It was awarded funding from Arts Council England in 2020 through the Elevate programme, for diverse-led arts organisations to build resilience.

theemmapress.com
hello@theemmapress.com
Birmingham, UK

CONTENTS

MENAGERIE

POEMS BY CHERYL PEARSON

ILLUSTRATIONS BY AMY EVANS

THE EMMA PRESS

Consider the Seahorse

We know him, some. Though he's never run under
a harvest moon, or lipped stale scones from a palm.

See how he moors to eelgrass with his tail. How he
breathes in salt, not sun. He's never mauled a weed

to stars or worn a shawl for cold. But he knows the mussel
and its labial folds, the jellyfish hauling its light. He sees

the blank-eyed great whites cruise like missiles. His body
is a question, but no one asks a thing. He blows out tinselled

strings of air, bends sweetly to his mate. His language has
no *run*, no *season*; his world has no corners. No apple

cores, or sugar cubes, but look: he rides the blue light
bareback. No bits or blinkers. No harnesses. No gates.

Octopus Tank, Torbay Aquarium

She flows away from the roof coming off –
the noise, the punch of light from the torch.

Unspools and re-ravels as we watch. First
fast. Then slow. A surge, and a gathering back.

A surge, and a gathering back. It lifts the hairs
on your arms and neck, makes a ballet of the tank.

I saw a ribbon of starlings once – they rose
and fell in that same way, tied and re-tied Rome

in a bow, and I thought the knot at their centre
must be God. Here is God again in this stranger,

the colour coursing her billow and flop like a weather map
crawling with storms. The current of command

from brain to brain, the crackle of travel between
all nine. As the crow flies, we are two hundred miles

from home. She is further. A thousand. An element.
Watch her fling one arm at the plate-glass, roll it

out like a rug – the kind you see in hallways,
long, embroidered – and see how the suckers

work like mouths. Opening. Closing. Imagine the hunger
of a creature with three hearts. For salt. For dark. For crab,

tossed in a tube whose catch she must pick. *To keep
her sharp,* the biologist tells us. *She has the intelligence*

of a three year old. He puts the roof on her blue-lit room,
and now she's a stream, all arms behind her, belly lighting

each mind like a bulb. And see how she tows the tube
to a corner. How once the moon towed the riddle of her.

Hermit

All along the sand, their improvised architecture
holds against weather and predator. Junked shells
and beach litter. Nut-hulls, mussels, and cans of cola

stripped of their shine by salt and exposure. This one
folds from a whelk-shell like a flower. That one hauls
an empty canister – camera-film, perhaps, or tub of glitter.

We tracked one crab in particular for weeks as she towed
a blue tumbler with a hairline fracture. When it ruptured,
she left her colourful scaffold behind, soft in her terror.

What is a poem? a teacher asked of her third graders.
A poem is an egg with a horse inside, answered a child.
Two things lifted from commonness. Rendered peculiar

in coming together. A fish spits up a leather trainer. A crab
drags a light bulb through marram grass. The world is stranger
than either you or I could guess. When the tide falters,

carcasses litter the ribbed sand, Cancer a mirror
overhead. Picked out in stars, their bright sister
works her pincers, draws the shell of the universe closer.

Lobsters

We stand in the tin stink of the harbour
watching the haul of pots and creels.
For lack of rock or wreck, the lobsters

climb each other, rubber-banded
for the restaurant tanks. A squadron.
A palaver. They bleed blue. Blue like

queens. How I'd love to see one spill
its skies without harm. A tropical wash
from plate and rivet. A flank of stars.

Their little mountain clatters. Bow-tied
waiters will give them names, propose
Marcel and Sebastian to diners. I take

two pills each morning, stab at calm.
Still there are many things to be sad
about. Single magpies. Thunderstorms.

You need to toughen up, the older doctor
said. I thought of lobsters, then. Small
fortresses. Still they suffer till they're dead.

A Comb Jellyfish Swallows
Another Comb Jellyfish

You see now how light travels. How language travels.
Like the lick of flame in an air balloon's silk. Illumination
from the inside out, a snake with its tail in the plug of its mouth.
How *swallow* turns in. How in consuming, is also consumed.
An open throat like a chimney full of sky, a pouring in
of light drunk in by light. There are one trillion things I do not know,
but I do know this: that entangled particles, even at a distance
of a thousand miles, are somehow linked. That scientists have proved
how an action on the particle quivering in France affects the one
in Yemen instantly. I think of you – far, tonight, from me, and sad.
And I am sad. And full of love, and all its light. And I watch the jellyfish,
which for a time is two, bear its selves away like a Chinese lantern,
its slow, radiant surge through sea. And I am glad to be human,
and confused every time by the line between beauty and catastrophe.

Great White

Sun on the water like broken glass,
and us dazzled mad in the boat, surrounded by ropes

and buckets of fish. *Their dead eyes,*
you say when they breach, and shiver. But we are also

animals. Despite our spiderplants
and Instagram accounts. Our credit cards

and watering cans. Yes, we'd be swallowed
like communion wafers. But I would sink a mallet

in a thousand skulls to feed
my daughter. I don't want them hauled to flood

a deck with red, a wristwatched arm.
Or boiled for soup. Teeth and light are the sharks' work.

Hunger's hunger. Watch them rise
in a veil of diamonds for a low gull, a swimmer.

Gold In The Lion

In 2005, veterinarians in Rome treated an arthritic lion with injections of gold.

They slip the needle in
while the sick animal is under.
Through living sun

to the muscle. Imagine
the crackle of lightning.
The blaze of light in the thigh.

You never noticed before
how the eyelid, rolled like a shutter,
discloses the eye. Warm

and gold as a Roman morning.
Imagine that, you say. And again,
with wonder, *Imagine*. Like

they're topping him up
with the smelted metals
he's made of. Like his blood

has always been crown-coloured,
shining. Already we are asking,
What next? This first fix

trailing a great hope. Tug-boat
with a liner large in its wake.
Its ballrooms, its lights.

A father with hands like root-
ginger. The brassy flash
of the plunger. The years after,

a luxury. I think of the vase
in the Japanese museum,
mended with gold along its faults,

its beauty in its repair. Like the father
tossing his daughter skyward.
Gold in his wrists. Gold in her hair.

Vixen

I light for the den of hindleggers.
The all-on-ups who flummox and fuss
at our slinkings-in. Keepers of cluckers
who make good our bellies, whose blood-
beaters patter like rain under feathers.

I follow my teeth to the red-to-come,
follow my own gold lights over grass.

Oh, bloodsmell! Oh, flush of rust! A flood
to loosen, a feast of salt when I open.

Quickquick I go, a lick of heat in the garden,
then gone. Six yellow eyes in the den-mouth
blinking off and on. *Mother*, and *hunger*;
the words are the same. I dance with risk
on black toes, fill the coops with snow.

I'd rob the world of bones to feed these
flames. Flicker, children. Flicker now.

Blue Mole

Piped from the clench of his mother's hind
on a full moon, a soft and suddenly living blue
winks on like a star in the dense dark.

He juggles milk and shadow for weeks,
learns his own spectacular shape –
the flashing blades, the nap of his pelt –

while his mother fills the burrow
with the smell of light. Who wouldn't want
a lick of that. Who wouldn't turn

their whole life towards it. When he goes,
he goes like a drill-bit rolled in suede,
eyes squinched tight against the earth's storm.

The first breach of the lawn, the first true air –
the nose shuffles off its ledge of dirt,
and the first star comes in, and settles there.

Hardangervidda

Lichen under tongues, still;
it was that quick. The boiled world split and caught
the spooked group in its lights.

Perhaps they found brief shelter under
the marvellous branches of their antlers.
The way a girl in a dress finds a tree in the rain
before she surrenders to translucence.

The lightning cut its teeth on a forest of blood.
Imagine the sound of their bodies
as they fell. A sigh as they peeled
out of formation. A pop and a spit as their fat
cooked where they stood.
A tangle of crowns in a brown field. A drift of smoke.

The metal lick of light that kissed
the metal in them: particles, perhaps,
from the same original star, an inevitable return

to lips and teeth. So that this, the collapse, is not a death,
but only those two old lovers meeting –
Here you are. After all these years.

And they leave, together. Not in the scavenging mouths
of foxes. Not in boxes in the scientists' cars.

n.b. In August 2016, over three hundred reindeer were killed by a
single lightning strike in Hardangervidda, Norway. Scientists explained
that reindeer tend to group together when spooked, and the
proximity of their bodies would have allowed the lightning to travel
through the herd unobstructed.

Hedgehog

Milk on flat moon comes
at dusk. Goodsmell meat.

Yes yes wings yes legs. Yes
fat silver, teeth. Trundle dim

for hunger. All dark I am. All
mouthmouth. Terror me to small.

Fox-piss bigger. Hoot and whoosh-
lights. Roll, then. Hide the tender.

Marius

In 2014, Marius, a young giraffe at Copenhagen
Zoo, was deemed unsuitable for breeding and
euthanised, before being publicly dissected.
Onlookers included a group of schoolchildren.

Laid out flat like a flag, or hunter's rug,
a human peg at each steaming corner.

See the heart which measures half a metre.
The black tongue. The kneeling children

lean in closer. Perhaps by now he'd be
bones on the plain. Hyena. Matchstick-

leg snapped clean. Perhaps he'd be
an hour older. The sky's a wound. *Look,*

says a keeper. His red hand dips to the gut
then flowers. *His last supper. Bread. Rye.*

In the corner, bluebottles tread a bucket
of parts. Already the acacia leaves are dry.

Peacock, Castle Howard

After the coast, this. Miles of brown
and rain. A two hour tickertape of trees.
The sun dazzles the wet. In the road's wells.
On the brown leaves. The only bold the blue
numbers restless in the fields, lambs sprayed
with a claim. We pull in for the castle shop,
thinking *local venison*, thinking *cheese*. Unkink
our backs in the car park, squint in the bright.
It's the high cry that prompts us to look – *here!*
here! All the world's colour on the rampart wall,
every fruit and jewel condensed. This is where
the summer went: blue sky, green grass, gold
flower to butter a throat. Lovelier for the park deer
and their brown crowns. Lovelier for the moat
of mud and moss. All cries and trailing silks,
like a killed queen mourning her head. See how
we stop for beauty. Stand in the mushroomy damp
and gape. On another planet, a football's kicked.
A chimney smokes. A pike tickles the face of a lake.

Magpie

Cock of the walk, of the square swept just for him
of studs of gum and plastic wrap.
This here's the city's kingpin. See how he struts,

dapper as Capone in his suit and spats.
Imagine a gun slung underwing, and cigarettes.
Moonshine in a monogrammed flask.

He keeps each gleam and glittering thing. A tax:
foil packets, ear-less pearls with silver backs,
and the double score of shining lid

and cream filched from the newsagent's mat.
And there his club of mobsters, glossy-tuxed,
rattling the statues with their gunfire chat.

I've seen them flatten pigeons in a mood.
I've seen them swagger, cocky, by the cat
who sleeps outside on the chip-shop bins,

dreaming of cod and feathered things
rounding out his old bones to fat. Then: *Scat!*
A toddler runs, all whoops and waving arms a-flap,

and the magpies lift in a sheet of black. For a moment,
the whole sky is dark as pitch, and then
they tack away. And the square is suddenly light, and plain,

like a storm has broken, done with its old havoc.

Flamingo

As though the gas was left on high, and a match
struck. And now the pale flames are licking at the glass

with long tongues of rosy light. Or else the yolk
of sunrise broke, and washed each bird in its blush,

the way red wine defies salt and sponge.
Some are soft; white lace held against a girl's cheek,

a peach growing down in the spring. Others blaze,
their doubles locked at a hot-pink foot.

All are exquisite. Their glad wings
sweeten the water.

The weight of it. All that beauty.
No wonder their flushed backs

sway underneath it. No wonder
the knobs of their knees are braced –

studs of colour, a bud on a branch,
the knot on the rope of a boat in the harbour.

Light as meringues. As delicate.
You describe them solely

in breakable language – eggshell, teacup,
hummingbird, wrist.

Do you think that you are capable
of grace like this? To step into cracked water,

and mend it? The vase of the throat opens.
The mouth brims with roses. How can the earth bear it?

Like love is borne; that other light
that burns, and cannot be extinguished.

Kingfisher

Falls like a rainbow wrapped
around a comet, a flash,
then gone –

a streak that shatters
the reflection
of itself and vanishes in a spool
of empty circles,
echoes travelling out and further out,

to whisper
to the earth and
thirsting roots,

and repeat
to the earth
and

thirsting roots.

What counsel is kept
in that roving dark, where striped fish
follow the current's pull
like the run
in a jumper, unravelling to a final spill
at cuff or collar?

The impossible comet re-enters
the atmosphere.

The air's electric,
a heart shocked back into rhythm,
riverwater streaming
from the tropical back,
a minnow
hanging from the cracked beak,

and if the sky was lacking a star,
the bird has replaced it – the fish
is tumbled by the gullet, yes,
but tonight

the moon will find the scales, a gift
in the branches, attend their lights
with her lights; perhaps

there is no better fate than this.

Fledgling

So still and empty of life on the path,
I can't imagine it being otherwise –

the slight release of its throat in the shell
as it dreamed of song, the tries of its beak

in the dark. Its eyes are the plum-blue
of bruises. I've seen its featherless translucence

in the plucked birds hugged by supermarket
plastic, cleaned of clucks for the plate. Its wings

are buds. When I was thirteen, this is how
I knew my breasts, at first. How I knew my shape

would bend and swell like riverwater
following its course. The broken shell rocks

at the tap of my toe. I remember hips
where I had been hipless, remember creaks

in the night as I grew. The way ships creak,
out at sea. How can this bird, limp and broken,

speak to me of a blue dress, my first kiss?
The first time I fell, yes; the first time I flew.

Owl Poem

Every flower is blue at night. Every field
of wheat. Navy sleeves the wood.

Two eyes marry the dark on a moonless branch.
Ring to ring, bright gold.

Their hoots are gently bowled. They gather
mice bones, moss.

What settles a grief? The owl knows. Blood
for a blue mood,

a hunger. See how they float. White and silent.
Snow falling on water.

ACKNOWLEDGEMENTS

Thank you to the following publications, in which some of these poems first appeared: *Frontier, The Lonely Crowd, The Interpreter's House, The High Window, Clear Poetry, Humanagerie* (Eibonvale Press), and *Diversifly* (Fair Acre Press).

ABOUT THE AUTHOR

Cheryl Pearson's first poetry collection, *Oysterlight*, was published by Pindrop Press in 2017. She won the 2016 Cheshire Prize for Literature and the 2017 Torbay Poetry Competition, and was highly commended in the 2017 Costa Short Story Awards. She lives in Manchester and spends her free time in the Peak District where she can usually be found climbing hills or drinking beer.

TWITTER: @CHERYLPEA
INSTAGRAM: @CHERYLPOIS

ABOUT THE ILLUSTRATOR

Amy Evans is an illustrator, living and working in the West Midlands. Between teaching and freelance work, she enjoys people-watching and sketch-booking away. She loves embracing traditional media, printing and mark-making, mixing hand-drawn elements with digital techniques to give energy, movement and character to the everyday.

WEBSITE: AMYLOUISEEVANS.CO.UK
INSTAGRAM: @AMYEVANSILLUSTRATION
TWITTER: @AMYINKYEVANS